AUSTIN
IMPRESSIONS

PHOTOGRAPHY BY LAURENCE PARENT
FOREWORD BY TEXAS STATE SENATOR KIRK WATSON

FARCOUNTRY
PRESS

Right: The buildings of Austin's business district rise above Lake Austin. From left, the four tallest are: 100 Congress Building (1986), One Congress Plaza (1987), San Jacinto Center (1987), and Frost Bank Tower (2001).

Below: Adopted in 1839, the Texas state flag—its red, blue, and white representing bravery, loyalty, and purity—inspired the nickname "Lone Star State." Texas is the only state that was recognized as an independent nation before statehood—during the Republic of Texas, 1836 to 1845.

Title page: Christmas lights brighten the Lady Bird Johnson Wildflower Center, which was founded in 1982 by the former First Lady and actress Helen Hayes.

Front cover: Sunset silhouettes the fountain at the Lyndon Baines Johnson Library and Museum. Johnson was the thirty-sixth president of the United States, from 1963 to 1969.

Back cover: A trip up Mount Bonnell, one of the highest points in Austin, rewards visitors with breathtaking views of Lake Austin.

ISBN 10: 1-56037-423-3
ISBN 13: 978-1-56037-423-7

© 2007 by Farcountry Press
Photography © 2007 by Laurence Parent

For more information about our books, write Farcountry Press, P.O. Box 5630, Helena, MT 59604; call (800) 821-3874; or visit www.farcountrypress.com.

Created, produced, and designed in the United States.
Printed in China.

12   11   10   09   08   07   1   2   3   4   5   6

FOREWORD | BY TEXAS STATE SENATOR KIRK WATSON

AUSTIN IS A CITY WITH STRIKING BEAUTY and a big personality. There's really no single adjective that adequately describes this unique place.

Photographer Laurence Parent, who has long resided in the dramatic Hill Country of Texas, turns his lens on Austin and captures in images what is sometimes difficult to convey in words.

At its heart, Austin is a verdant landscape of hills, trees, and water. Explorers described a beautiful land rising on the edge of the Balcones Escarpment, which is where the Texas Hill Country begins. They also reported the stunning power of the Colorado River and the natural springs that today are the Barton Springs Pool, what many consider to be the soul of the city.

Settlers founded the village of Waterloo here in 1837, and the town was selected as the capital and renamed Austin in 1839 in honor of "Father of Texas" Stephen F. Austin.

Today, we Austinites can still enjoy the area's natural beauty. Year round, we run, walk, and bike on the Town Lake Hike and Bike Trail—the "front yard" of our downtown area. We canoe, kayak, and compete in rowing sports on the Colorado River, which flows past Austin's downtown.

Austin has set aside thousands of acres as preserve and park land to protect its natural resources for future generations. The Lady Bird Johnson Wildflower Research Center is an oasis of breathtaking native plants. A lengthy ribbon of rugged, undeveloped Hill Country, the Barton Creek Greenbelt extends through the city, attracting hikers, mountain bikers, kayakers, and rock climbers. And although manmade, the Highland Lakes, created by dams along the Colorado River to stem flooding, are sparkling jewels that enhance the natural beauty of the Hill Country.

Parent's photographs reveal another side of Austin—its rich culture and strong musical tradition. Known as the Live Music Capital of the World, Austin boasts a variety of clubs, such as the Continental Club on South Congress, and honky-tonks, such as the Broken Spoke.

Downtown has become a twenty-four-hour, bustling mix of people who live in the urban core, work in one of the strongest local business communities in the country, enjoy fine dining in the Warehouse District, visit the Children's Museum or Austin Museum of Art, party in the famous Sixth Street entertainment district, and enjoy productions at the restored Paramount Theatre.

Above: When sculptor Pompeo Coppini designed this statue of Stephen F. Austin (1793 to 1836), it was to stand where Congress Avenue meets the Colorado River, with Austin's hand pointing to the city named for the "Father of Texas." But today, the sculpture rises above Austin's grave in the Texas State Cemetery. The town of Waterloo was renamed "Austin" three years after the colonizer's death.

Facing page: Town Lake, created by a dam on the Colorado River, is among several features that earn Austin the distinction of being called "a city within a park."

Downtown is also home to a large population of Mexican free-tailed bats, which reside under the Congress Avenue Bridge. At dusk, they darken the sky as they fly out from under the bridge to eat insects—to the delight of hundreds of people who gather to witness the spectacle.

Historic buildings and museums, such as the Lyndon Baines Johnson Library and Museum, the Bob Bullock State History Museum, and Austin City Hall, are all unique attractions. The historic Governor's Mansion is located downtown and continues to be the official Governor's residence. A short trip outside of Austin leads to the LBJ Ranch, the former home and final resting place of President Lyndon Johnson, who grew up in the Hill Country and represented the Austin area in the U.S. Congress.

Austin is also home of the University of Texas. The UT Longhorns are known not only for successful athletic teams but for high-quality educational and scientific research programs. The city's other colleges, such as St. Edward's University in South Austin, have also educated generations of Austinites.

Ultimately, a city is defined by its people. We Austinites are an open-minded group, and we encourage efforts to keep this place unique. This sentiment is demonstrated in what is arguably the most popular bumper sticker here, a plea to "Keep Austin Weird."

Indeed, there are many faces of Austin. And photographer Laurence Parent has created a portrait of Austin that is picture perfect.

Above: The Texas Governor's Mansion, dating from 1856, is the oldest continuously occupied executive residence west of the Mississippi. During structural restoration of the Greek-revival edifice from 1979 to 1982, the interior was refurbished and furnished with nineteenth-century American antiques.

Right: During the time of the Republic of Texas, France sent a *chargé d'affaires* to represent its interests, especially in the cotton market. Jean Pierre Isidore Alphonse Dubois de Seligny's old-world ways did not sit well with the republic's free-spirited Texans, but he did leave behind the charming 1841 home that today is the French Legation Museum.

Left: Pennybacker Bridge carries Loop 360—officially the Capital of Texas Highway—over Lake Austin. Percy V. Pennybacker, Jr. (1895 to 1963), a native Texan, was a bridge designer for the Texas Highway Department who pioneered welded-metal bridges.

Below: Fine homes perch on the hills above Lake Austin.

above: Beyond this entrance, twenty-two stories of offices await inside the sunset-
ed granite 100 Congress Building.

ight: An obelisk honors state winners of the Medal of Honor in the Texas State
Cemetery, where many notable Texans are buried.

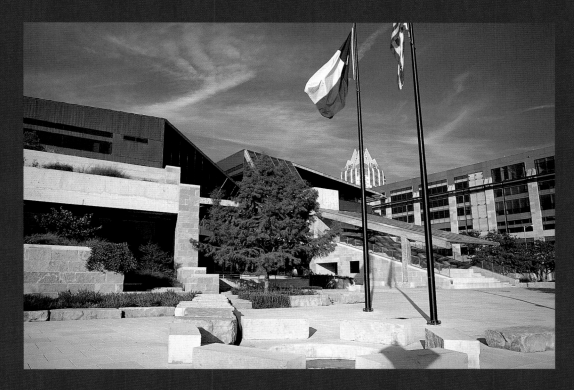

Above: Austin City Hall, opened in 2004, was planned as a four-story gathering place for government and public functions and includes an outdoor stage on the plaza.

Left: Around Austin, more than fifty miles of trails course through natural greenbelts, such as this one along Town Lake.

Right: Austin was named the capital city in 1839, and the Renaissance revival–style Texas State Capitol was completed in 1888. Approximately 4,000 train-cars' worth of Texas pink granite was used to construct the exterior.

Below: The dome above the capitol's rotunda rises to 311 feet, 15 feet higher than that of the United States Capitol.

Above: Opened in 1911 as the Majestic Theatre to show silent films, the Paramount Theatre for the Performing Arts was glamorized in the 1930s before becoming a B-movie house after World War II. In 1975, it was restored and opened as a venue for live performances.

Left: The Bob Bullock Texas State History Museum, championed by two-term Lieutenant Governor Bob Bullock, opened in 2001, two years after the statesman's death. Facilities include an IMAX theater, interactive exhibits, and multimedia presentations.

PHOTO BY RICHARD CUMMINGS

Right: The Oasis restaurant, the self-proclaimed "sunset capital of Texas," offers spectacular views of Lake Travis.

Below: Austin rock climbers head west of town to Enchanted Rock State Natural Area, along with backpackers, hikers, picnickers, bird watchers, and star gazers.

Above: Sportswriter D. A. Frank first labeled the University of Texas football team "the Longhorns" in 1904, and the name stuck. The first live mascot, Bevo I, appeared during the 1916 season; it wasn't until 1966 that the mascot became a feature of every game.

Left: Burnt-orange and white school colors are prominent on the home side of the University of Texas football field during a football game.

Above: Last light colors the geometry of Congress Avenue's business-block facades.

Right: Unusual silver-blue glass covers the Frost Bank Tower (tallest building at right), with the pointed crown alone using an acre's worth of it.

Above: Rio Grand takes to the stage at Graham Central Station, a popular mega-club in Pflugerville, a suburb of Austin, that features a country bar, rock bar, dance club, karaoke bar, and more.
PHOTO COURTESY OF GARY EATON, ℅ GRAHAM CENTRAL STATION, AUSTIN

Left: Trick Pony puts on a wild show at Graham Central Station, which opened in 2005.
PHOTO COURTESY OF GARY EATON, ℅ GRAHAM CENTRAL STATION, AUSTIN

Above: Barton Creek Greenbelt stretches eight miles and offers fishing, swimming, mountain biking, and hiking amid lush vegetation.

Right: Hamilton Pool Nature Preserve, just outside Austin in Travis County, includes this welcoming waterfall and swimming hole.

Above: Texas longhorn cattle are believed to be the result of crossbreeding between Spanish and English cattle that were brought here. Their horns can extend as much as eight feet from tip to tip.

Left: Since 1930, the Steiner family has run Capitol Saddlery, offering custom saddles, boots, and leather goods—at one time, selling some saddle designs through the Sears, Roebuck and Montgomery Ward catalogs. Here, craftsman Lance Broussard puts the finishing touches on one of his saddles.

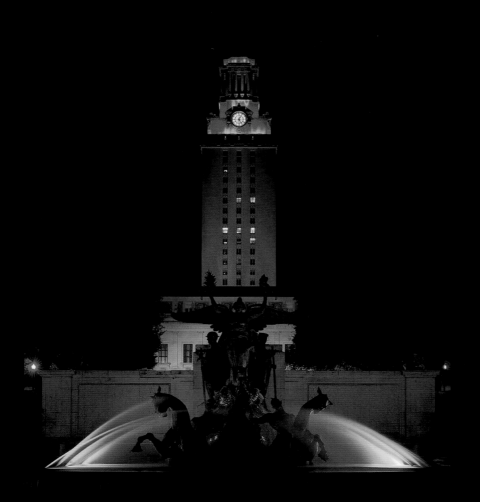

Above: Orange and white lighting patterns on the University of Texas Main Building Tower signal various achievements and awards. This design indicates a football victory.

Right: The Lyndon Baines Johnson Library and Museum—opened in 1971—includes this fountain and covers thirty acres of the University of Texas campus.

Above: In East Austin, George Washington Carver Museum and Cultural Center opened in 1979 and was named for the Tuskegee University–founding scientist who applied his discipline to food-processing and household products.

Left: An unnamed stream ambles among cypress trees in Milton Reimers Ranch Park, which lies along the Pedernales River in Travis County thirty miles southwest of Austin. Visitors enjoy mountain biking, world-class rock climbing, and fishing—as well as tranquil scenes like this one.

Right: Congress Avenue rolls through South Austin and downtown to the Texas State Capitol.

Below: The Lorenzo de Zavala State Archives and Library Building, just east of the capitol, dates from 1961. Its name honors a former governor of the State of Mexico who moved with his family to Texas in 1824 and was elected vice president of the Republic of Texas in 1836, serving several months until his death.

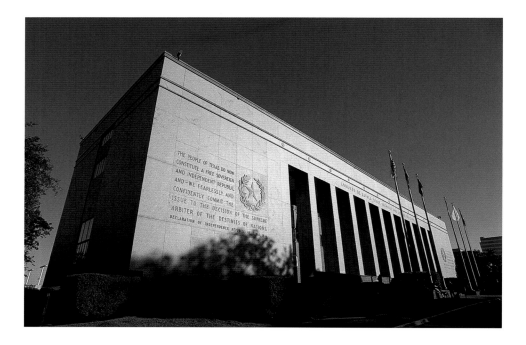

Above: West of Austin, Lyndon B. Johnson National Historical Park includes the president's boyhood home, where he lived from age five until graduating from high school at age fifteen.

Left: Visitors to the historical park can pay their respects at LBJ's grave in the family cemetery.

Right: "SoCo," the South Congress Avenue district, features quirky shops with chic and unusual clothing and décor items.

Below: In 2006, the Gibson Guitar Corporation, headquartered in Nashville, sponsored the "Austin GuitarTown" public arts project, with local artists and celebrities decorating ten-foot-tall fiberglass guitars for display throughout the city. Proceeds from the sales were donated to the Health Alliance for Austin Musicians, Austin Museum of Art, American Youthworks, and Austin Children's Museum.

Left: A fiery sunrise silhouettes Austin's skyli

Below: After the Congress Avenue Bridge over
decided to move in. From March until Octo
750,000 and 1.5 million of them—forming
Crowds gather at sunset to watch the creatu

© MERLIN D. TUTTLE, BAT CONSERVATION INTERNATION

Above: A kayaker paddles the rapids of Barton Creek.

Right: The Barton Creek Greenbelt includes several small waterfalls, over which the stream flows to join the Colorado River at Town Lake.

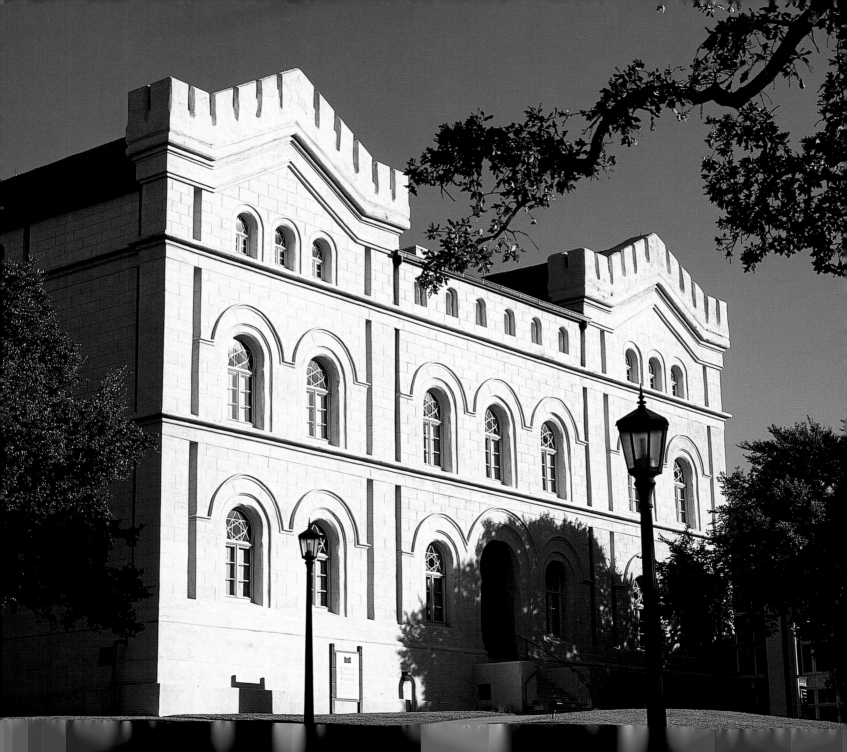

Above: The Neill-Cochran House, a family home from 1855 until 1958, today is a museum operated by the National Society of the Colonial Dames of America. Period rooms exhibit furnishings of 1700 through 1900: colonial, empire, rococo, revival, and Victorian.

Left: Built in 1856 and 1857, the medieval revival–style General Land Office is the oldest state office building in Texas from which public lands once were managed. Today it houses historical exhibits and serves as the Capitol Visitor Center.

Above: Blues guitarist Stevie Ray Vaughan (1954 to 1990) often performed in Austin, leading to the 1994 placement of this sculpture at Auditorium Shores along Town Lake. Visitors flock to the site to pay homage to Vaughan's legendary talent.

Right: Three acres in size and fed by underground springs, Barton Springs Pool is a welcome place to cool off. Legend has it that state legislators have informally drafted laws here, and actor Robert Redford said that at age five he learned to swim in the pool while visiting an Austin relative.

Left: The lights of downtown Austin draw bands of color across Town Lake.

Below: Since 1993, Chuy's Hula Hut has served "Mexonesian" fusion cuisine above Lake Austin, offering such intriguing treats as Hawaiian fajitas and mango margaritas.

Above: The architectural details of the Texas State Capitol extend to the ornate hinges of its massive entrance doors. Cast in Connecticut and measuring eight inches by eight inches, each set of bronze hinges weighs more than

Above: The Austin Museum of Arts–Laguna Gloria is housed in a Mediterranean-style villa that was built in 1916 on land Stephen F. Austin originally chose as his home site. Clara Driscoll, the "savior of the Alamo," deeded the building, her former home, to the Texas Fine Arts Association in 1943. Laguna Gloria presents eight to ten exhibitions each year, mostly twentieth-century American art.

Left: This original 1916 rock trail at the Austin Museum of Arts–Laguna Gloria leads to the Temple of Love, a historical replication of a classic gazebo built for Clara Driscoll.

Above: Frost Bank Tower's glass exterior takes on subtle hues at dusk.

Right: Bluebonnets are the state flower of Texas. Wildflower lovers can follow several Bluebonnet Trails in the Austin area and throughout the state.

Left: Formed in 1939 by the construction of the Tom Miller Dam, Lake Austin is used for flood control, electrical power generation, and recreation—and it's a great place to watch the sun set.

Below: Canoeists ply the waters of Town Lake. Docks were built on the lak to promote rowing and other family water sports.

above: Hamilton Creek cuts through limestone outcroppings in Hamilton Pool Preserve en route to the Pedernales River.

right: Littlefield House on the University of Texas campus today hosts special presidential functions. It was built in 1893 as the home of cattle baron and banker George Littlefield and his wife, Alice. The couple, who never had children of their own, supported the university throughout their lives, and Alice willed UT the Victorian mansion upon her death in 1935.

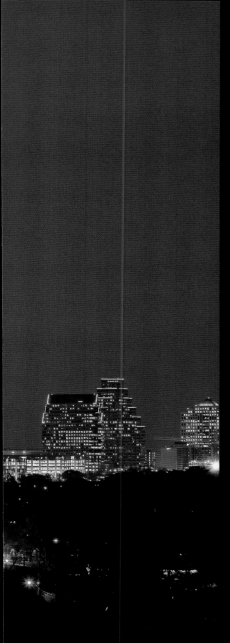

Above: A pecan tree, the state tree of Texas, is caught in winter's grip in Travis County. The Lone Star State produces the most native pecans among the fifty states, with Georgia growing the most hybrid pecans.

Left: Zilker Park, decorated here for Christmas, is named in honor of Andrew Jackson "Colonel Andy" Zilker (1858 to 1934), the city's first Coca-Cola bottler and donor of the park's 350-some acres.

Right: Children give the shore of Town Lake some close scrutiny.

Below: Whole Foods Market's downtown store and corporate headquarters are located a few blocks from where the first Whole Foods store opened in 1980.

Above: The Broken Spoke, founded in 1964, advertises itself as "the last of the true Texas dancehalls" where you can two-step to live, big-name, honky-tonk bands—and possibly bump into Willie Nelson stopping in for some chicken-fried steak.

Left: The Continental Club in SoCo has been around since 1957. It is known as the "granddaddy of all local music venues" in Austin, and was one of Stevie Ray Vaughan's regular stops.

Above: In 1933, Pompeo Coppini designed the Littlefield Fountain in front of Main Mall at the University of Texas. The fountain is named after George Littlefield, whose trust funded its construction as a tribute to war heroes.

Right: This placid fountain accents the Lyndon Baines Johnson Library and Museum.

Above: Seeping water nourishes these ferns clinging to a canyon wall in Milton Reimers Ranch Park.

Left: Onion Creek's lower falls adorn McKinney Falls State Park, which was established on land Thomas F. McKinney settled in the early 1850s. McKinney had arrived in Texas three decades earlier as one of Stephen Austin's original 300 colonists.

Above: "The Drag," along the University of Texas' western edge, is a portion of Guadalupe Street—pronounced gwa-da-loop by Austinites.

Facing page: The Driskill Hotel features a Historic Wing (1886) and a Traditional Wing (1929), with a total of 188 luxurious rooms and suites.

Left: Located alongside Town Lake in downtown Austin, the Lester E. Palmer Events Center has received numerous architectural awards. Palmer was the mayor of Austin from 1961 to 1967.

Below: German-born sculptor Elisabet Ney (1833 to 1907) and her Scottish husband, Dr. Edmund Montgomery, moved to Texas in 1873 and influenced the establishment of state universities and the Texas Fine Arts Association. Today Ney's studio, initially preserved by her friends, is one of the state's oldest museums.

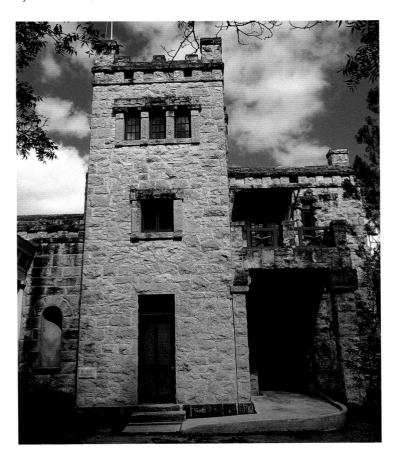

ust west of central downtown Austin, the rehabilitated
Warehouse District offers fine dining, live music, and
concert halls a bit more upscale than those in SoCo.

Parents and educators created the first Austin Children's
Museum as a traveling "museum without walls" in
1983. It settled into a building four years later, and in

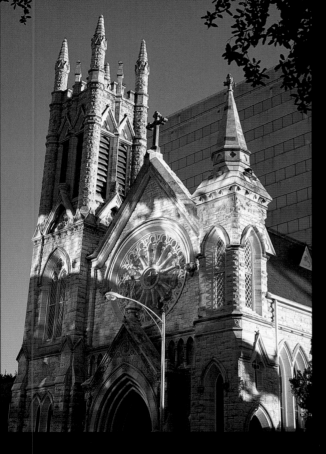

St. Mary Cathedral's cornerstone was laid in 1872. Congregant Nicholas Clayton designed the structure, which was restored inside and out during the early 2000s.

At the Alamo Drafthouse in the Warehouse District, patrons can watch their films either from theater seats or from bench-style tables where casual dining is available throughout the show—ordered by hand-written notes and served by silent waiters.

Left: The bronze *Lone Star* sculpture at the Bob Bullock State History Museum stands thirty-five feet tall, setting the scene for the "story of Texas" that awaits inside.

Below: Established as a small academy in 1878, St. Edward's University became a full-fledged university in 1925. Today the Catholic school serves 4,000 students. Seen here is the Main Building, which burned down and was rebuilt— all in 1903.

Facing pages: Austin's streets are relatively quiet as dawn breaks.

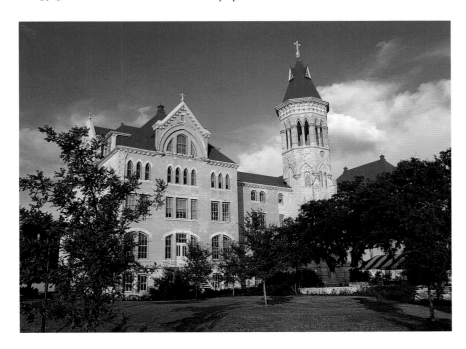

LAURENCE PARENT was born and raised in New Mexico. After receiving a petroleum engineering degree at the University of Texas at Austin in 1981, he practiced engineering for six years before becoming a full-time freelance photographer and writer specializing in landscape, travel, and nature subjects. His photos appear in numerous calendars. His many article and photo credits include *National Geographic Traveler*, *Outside*, *Backpacker*, *Newsweek*, and the *New York Times*. Laurence contributes regularly to regional publications such as *Texas Highways*, *Texas Monthly*, *New Mexico Magazine*, and *Texas Parks & Wildlife*. He has had more than thirty books published.

He makes his home in the Austin area with his wife Patricia and two children.

Right: Bull Creek Greenbelt serves up a restful summer sight.